DECEPTION
Reality TV

Jordan Smith

Publishing Credits

Rachelle Cracchiolo, M.S.Ed., *Publisher*
Conni Medina, M.A.Ed., *Managing Editor*
Nika Fabienke, Ed.D., *Series Developer*
June Kikuchi, *Content Director*
John Leach, *Assistant Editor*
Courtney Roberson, *Senior Graphic Designer*

TIME and the TIME logo are registered trademarks of TIME Inc. Used under license.

Image Credits: p.6, p.30 Kathy Hutchins/Shutterstock; p.7 (top) CBS Photo Archive/Getty Images; pp.8–9 Monty Brinton/CBS Photo Archive via Getty Images; pp.10–11 Bill Inoshita/CBS Photo Archive via Getty Images; pp.14–15 Barcroft Images/Barcroft Media via Getty Images; p.16 S. Bukley/Shutterstock; p.17 (top) Paul Smith/Featureflash/Shutterstock; p.17 (bottom) Joe Seer/Shutterstock; p.18, pp.20–21, p.29 FOX via Getty Images; p.19 Sterling Munksgard/Shutterstock; pp.22–23 Joe Russo/imageSpace/Sipa USA/Newscom; p.26 Preston Mack/Zuma Press/Newscom; p.27 Debby Wong/Shutterstock; p.31 Richard Shotwell/Invision/AP; p.37 Lev Radin/Shutterstock; p.48 Tania Volobueva/Shutterstock; all other images from iStock and/or Shutterstock.

All companies and products mentioned in this book are registered trademarks of their respective owners or developers and are used in this book strictly for editorial purposes; no commercial claim to their use is made by the author or the publisher.

Library of Congress Cataloging-in-Publication Data
Names: Smith, Jordan, 1993 March 6- author.
Title: Deception : reality tv / Jordan Smith.
Description: Huntington Beach, CA : Teacher Created Materials, [2018] | Includes index.
Identifiers: LCCN 2017056437 (print) | LCCN 2018013016 (ebook) | ISBN 9781425854782 (e-book) | ISBN 9781425850029 (softcover)
Subjects: LCSH: Reality television programs--United States--Juvenile literature.
Classification: LCC PN1992.8.R43 (ebook) | LCC PN1992.8.R43 S63 2018 (print)
| DDC 791.45/6--dc23
LC record available at https://lccn.loc.gov/2017056437

Teacher Created Materials
5301 Oceanus Drive
Huntington Beach, CA 92649-1030
www.tcmpub.com
ISBN 978-1-4258-5002-9

Table of Contents

Reality...Or Is It?

When you turn on the television, what kinds of shows are you drawn to? Choices range from comedies, dramas, game shows, documentaries, sports, and more. Then, there is a category of television that people may not admit to watching—reality TV. Celebrities have been created by this **genre**. Some reality stars are talented musicians, singers, chefs, home renovators, and hair stylists. Others are famous simply for sharing every aspect of their lives with the public.

Many of us are drawn to reality TV. We check out what our favorite reality star is up to. Or we root and vote for our favorite contestants on competition shows.

A common **misconception** is that reality TV is only about following the **lavish** lives of the rich and famous. But it is much more than this. Whether your interests lean toward music, baking, or fashion design, reality TV has something for everyone.

A Long History

Reality TV has been around almost as long as TVs. The television was first shown to the public in 1927. The first reality show debuted in 1948.

Too Much TV?

A recent study measured the amount of time teens watch television. The average kid aged 12 to 17 watches over 15 hours of TV per week. Teens spend more time watching TV than doing any other activity except sleeping.

The Joke That Started It All

Reality TV is not a new **phenomenon**; it has been around since the 1940s. One of the first reality shows was *Candid Camera*. It showed people taking cameras to the streets to capture practical jokes. *Candid Camera* **aired** on and off from 1948 to 2014.

From playing jokes to sending in funny videos, people were doing anything to get on TV. Then, in 1973, *An American Family* **broadcast** the life of a wealthy family in California. This gave the rest of the United States a look into a world most were not familiar with. This was the start of the most well-known type of reality TV. Today, many channels air a variety of reality shows.

A New Kind of Show

An American Family made the Loud family famous. The show started as a **documentary** about the Santa Barbara, California, family. It ended up launching a new **era** of television. Different from other shows of its time, it had no host or interviews. This led to many later shows in this format, such as *Chrisley Knows Best* (above).

Allen Funt, the creator and first host of *Candid Camera*

The Not-So-Real World

MTV's *The Real World* started in 1992. It was different in format from *An American Family*. Seven people were chosen from thousands of **applicants**. These seven strangers lived together in a house for months. But viewers saw only 13 edited, drama-filled episodes.

Altering Reality

One of the realities of reality TV is that not all the action that happens during filming can be shown. It must be **condensed**. **Footage** is shot and often edited in a way that adds drama.

In *Survivor*, people are forced to compete with one another to survive in the wild. They also must vote for one of their castmates to go home each week. What people may not realize is that each **season** actually takes place over 39 days. It is then edited and condensed, giving viewers only a brief look at what went on. This show was one of the first **unscripted** competition shows, and it had extremely high ratings during its first season in 2000. It did so well that many networks copied the format, launching shows such as *The Amazing Race* and *American Idol*.

Race for Cash

The Amazing Race premiered in 2001. Teams of two work together to travel the world and complete challenges. Team members have different skill sets, making some challenges easier for some teams. Teams compete for a grand prize of $1 million.

contestants on *Survivor*

ow enough.

tted
ying
pace
cities
er the
ivers.

range
stors.

vagen
s with
tt, an
rator.

pple's
ailing
uxing.

500m
velop
g cars.

Editors as Storytellers

Video editors for TV take on the role of storytellers. They take footage that was shot over a long period of time and cut it to fit a certain amount of time. The show also has to be edited in a way that engages the audience.

For most of these countri il is the ain source of

On *Survivor*, competitors are left in **exotic** locations and must survive the elements—and challenges—to win prize money. Everyone is split into teams called *tribes*. Tribe members must work together to win. But everyone is also competing against one another. When a tribe loses a challenge, one of its members is "voted off the island." In the end, only one person wins $1 million.

Contestants usually form **alliances** to advance. However, a certain amount of deception is involved in *Survivor*. People lie and sometimes betray their alliances to win. Building relationships is an important part of the game. The people who are voted off will ultimately choose the winner.

Themes

Each season of *Survivor* has a different theme and location. The show has been filmed in places such as Kenya, China, and Australia. Themes include "All-Stars" and "Game Changers," where contestants from previous seasons come back to compete for the top spot.

A Major Following

A long-running show, such as *Survivor*, usually has serious fans. There are blogs about the show—some even claim to know who will win before the show airs. *Entertainment Weekly* magazine extensively covers the show. Its radio station even has a *Survivor* segment, where the person voted off that week calls in and talks about his or her experience.

Find Your Passion

Many people have **hobbies** that their families and friends do not share. That's not a problem in the world of reality TV! Just tune in to any number of shows about your favorite hobbies and immerse yourself in someone else's world.

If you like singing and dancing, you have a variety of shows to watch. If you like cooking and baking, watch any Food Network reality program. Many are competition shows. You can watch people **hone** their **culinary** crafts and pick up some tips to try in the kitchen. If you're creative and artsy, check out reality shows about fashion design, arts and crafts, home renovation, or interior design. And that just skims the surface of what is out there. There truly is an endless amount of reality TV!

Hundreds of Shows

From *Survivor's* humble beginning to today, more and more reality shows are being made. Some are big hits and last for a long time. Others, such as *Celebrity Boxing*, only last for a short time. There are hundreds of reality shows to choose from. See the different categories below.

24 shows	74 shows	30 shows	39 shows	35 shows
Competing for prizes	Talent competitions	Dating & love	Family	Autobiographical

THINK LINK

> What hobbies do you have that you do not share with your peers?

> What shows could you watch to get more information about these hobbies?

> Besides being about your favorite hobbies, what is the appeal of these reality TV shows?

18 shows	28 shows	44 shows	8 shows
Stunts and Gags	Life improvement	Businesses and careers	Hidden camera and trickery

More Than a Judge

In real life, finding a hobby is easy, but finding a **mentor** can be hard. Mentors provide help, instruction, and support.

Competition shows often feature celebrity judges who add to the shows' appeal. These judges can double as mentors because they are **prominent** voices in industries such as music or food. They are there not only to judge but also to offer advice and guidance to contestants. These mentors give hopeful future stars the help they need to improve their skills.

Famous Voices

Although coaches on the singing competition *The Voice* are famous singers themselves, they also bring in outside help. These mentors from the music industry offer tips and points of view that are different from the judges. Superstars such as Tom Jones and Jennifer Hudson have appeared on the show.

Competition shows often run footage of the rehearsals prior to the main show. Audiences can see how the judges interact with the contestants. They can also see how the contestants have improved thanks to the advice of the judges and other famous mentors. Sometimes, judges perform with the contestants, too!

host and coaches of
The Voice UK season 6

Supporting Role

Harry Connick Jr. was a judge on *American Idol*. He also served as a mentor to the aspiring singers. He made sure to know what all the contestants were singing in order to give them helpful feedback. In an interview with *Billboard*, Connick said, "Honesty, preparation, and spontaneity are the keys," when asked about being a judge.

Reality Roles

There are different types of people who appear on reality shows. Hosts, producers, and judges all play important roles in the success—and failure—of contestants. Sometimes, these people have more than one role.

Judge

Judges play an important role in competition shows. Before the audience can weigh in, the judges often handpick the contestants. The judges are usually knowledgeable about singing or dancing, so fans can look to them to guide their choices for a winner. Julianne Hough is a judge on *Dancing with the Stars*. Prior to this, she was one of the dancers who won the competition with her celebrity partners.

Producer

All shows have producers. This job covers a range of things: creating the concept of the show, pitching the idea, and overseeing filming and production. Jeff Probst is a well-known producer on *Survivor*. He is also the show's host.

Host

Competition shows often have hosts who support contestants and give them information about what is to come. They also engage the audience and fill them in on anything they need to know. Ryan Seacrest was the famous host of *American Idol*. He is also the producer of many famous reality shows, including *Keeping Up with the Kardashians*.

Mystery Meal

Young adults compete for the top spot on *Chopped Junior*. The contestants are given ingredients that they must use to make tasty meals. The challenge is that the ingredients provided would not ordinarily be cooked together, and contestants must use all their ingredients to get the best possible score.

Not Just for Adults

There are many reality shows that feature talented kids and teens. These programs prove that no matter people's ages, they can follow their dreams and passions. Audiences are amazed as these talented young chefs, singers, and designers take center stage.

Serving Up Success

There are several cooking shows where kids and teenagers serve up delicious and complicated dishes. Shows such as *MasterChef Junior* and *Junior Bake Off* put young chefs in the heat of competition. They learn the tricks of the trade from the judges along the way. The kids come from different places but become fast friends, united by their knowledge and culinary **prowess**. Even though they are competing, they support one another.

Tasty Treats

Pastry chef Duff Goldman hosts the *Kids Baking Championship*. Young bakers compete in a series of challenges for a chance to win $10,000 and have their winning cakes showcased in Goldman's famous bakery, Charm City Cakes. Talk about a sweet way to work on your baking skills!

In *MasterChef Junior,* the pint-sized chefs are remarkably good at what they do. Each week, they receive a challenge to make a dish that most viewers know nothing about. As the show progresses, judges eliminate contestants until one is crowned "Master Chef."

Junior Bake Off is a British baking show featuring kids with a passion for pastries. The contestants bake a variety of complex sweets each week. The young bakers get some serious support from culinary pros. These contestants will inspire you to try your hand at whipping up something in

Kitchen Masters

MasterChef Junior contestants must prove they know their way around the kitchen. Challenges may include a technical skill, such as precise cutting. Sometimes, these challenges seem impossible. For example, the young chefs may be asked to re-create a recipe from something they simply tasted.

ow enough.

ted
ing
ace
ities
the
yers.

ange
tors.

agen
with
t, an
rator.

ople's
ailing
xing.

500m
velop
cars.

Double Desserts

In *Junior Bake Off*, bakers are challenged to make two recipes each week. One is a "technical challenge" to see how well they can **perfect** a recipe, such as chocolate chip cookies. The other is the "showstopper challenge," where contestants are given a more difficult dessert to make their own.

For most of these count

A Passion for Fashion

There are also competition shows for kids and teens who are interested in **textiles**. Fashion guru Tim Gunn serves as a mentor on *Project Runway* and *Project Runway: Junior*. On *Project Runway*, adult contestants must design outfits based on a theme. With a limited amount of time and materials, they are forced to get very creative. Celebrity judges, including producer and host Heidi Klum, **critique** their creations.

An **offshoot** of *Project Runway* is *Project Runway: Junior*, where budding designers from ages 13 to 17 show their skills. The formats of the shows are similar—the only difference is the age of the contestants. The young designers get to work with famous fashion designers and models. These reality shows prove that it is never too early to pursue your passion.

Tim Gunn

Endless Opportunities

The winner of *Project Runway: Junior* receives many prizes. He or she gets a scholarship to go to a fashion school in California. The winner also gets a home sewing studio and a feature in *Seventeen* magazine.

Heidi Klum

Wild Outfits

Project Runway contestants have been asked to make some strange outfits over the years. One season, they made a uniform for postal service workers. During another season, they designed matching outfits for people and their dogs.

Who Has Your Vote?

On some competition shows, viewers participate by voting for their favorite contestants. Talent competition shows, such as *American Idol*, *The Voice*, and *Dancing with the Stars*, rely on audience votes. Including the viewers in the outcome of who stays and who goes often results in higher ratings for the shows.

These shows air footage of the contestants' backstories. Many of these stories are very **compelling**. When contestants are introduced, you learn a little bit about them. Maybe you can identify with something they are going through or struggling with, or maybe they live in the same region as you do. Knowing more than how well they sing or dance tends to influence your voting behavior. It is likely to affect your viewing behavior, too. Each week, chances are high that viewers will check in to see how their favorites are doing.

Changing Technology

Viewers used to vote for their favorite contestants by dialing a number on their landline phones. Now, audiences can weigh in online and via call, text, and even tweet.

In 2012, more votes were tallied during the *American Idol* finale than in the presidential election. To vote for president, people must go to a polling place and cast a ballot or mail in a ballot. Votes for *American Idol* could be cast much more easily—by phone, computer, or text. Because of this, many people were able to vote more than once.

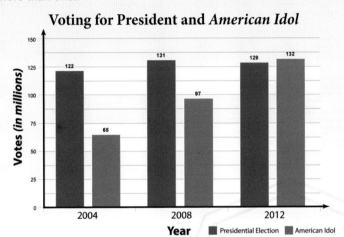

Voting for President and *American Idol*

Votes (in millions) vs Year

- 2004: 122 (Presidential Election), 65 (American Idol)
- 2008: 131 (Presidential Election), 97 (American Idol)
- 2012: 129 (Presidential Election), 132 (American Idol)

Legend: Presidential Election, American Idol

> Why do you think more votes were cast for *American Idol* than president in 2012?

> How could voting through personal devices change voter turnout for the presidential election? What problems could it cause?

American Idol

American Idol is one of the most popular competition shows ever. The singing contest aired from 2002 to 2016 on Fox. It returned in 2018 on a new network, ABC.

This popular reality show created musical superstars. Each season, thousands of contestants auditioned for the chance to go to Hollywood. The contestants **vied** to become the next American Idol. Hopeful singers battled it out each week in front of a panel of judges. Viewers at home decided their fates. The contestants got coaching from mentors. They faced new challenges on every episode. Often, they had to sing a song from a set genre or era.

Famous Idols

Kelly Clarkson (right) won the first season of *American Idol*. Carrie Underwood was also a winner on the show. Other contestants did not win but went on to have successful musical careers. They include Clay Aiken, Adam Lambert, Chris Daughtry, and Oscar® winner Jennifer Hudson.

Carrie Underwood

Four Little Words

Before they were officially on the show, contestants on *American Idol* hoped to hear four little words. If you made the cut, you were told, "You're going to Hollywood," and handed a golden ticket.

Dance to the Top

If dancing is more your style, there are plenty of fast feet to follow. *So You Think You Can Dance* has dancers compete for top spots by auditioning for judges. The selected dancers then compete in a round called "The Academy." From there, the top 10 dancers are chosen, and it is the audience's turn to weigh in with votes. The top 10 dancers get paired with all-stars. These professional dancers serve as mentors, helping contestants stay in the contest week after week.

Dancers perform in pairs each week. Contestants show off their skills in a variety of dance styles. Then, the audience votes for who will become America's Favorite Dancer.

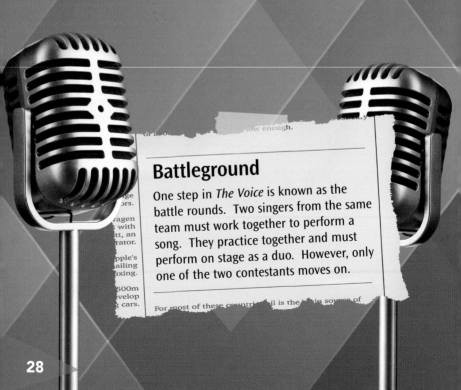

Battleground

One step in *The Voice* is known as the battle rounds. Two singers from the same team must work together to perform a song. They practice together and must perform on stage as a duo. However, only one of the two contestants moves on.

Styles of Dance

Dancers bring their talents from all types of dance to *So You Think You Can Dance*. Ballroom and salsa are traditional types of dance that you might expect to see on the show, but contestants also show off tap-dance routines and hip-hop moves.

Dancing into the Spotlight

Dancing with the Stars is a popular show that showcases the dancing talent of celebrities, athletes, and reality stars. Each season, stars are paired with professional dancers, and they battle it out every week.

The pro dancers teach routines to their partners, who may not have any dancing experience. Each week, pairs are challenged to learn a certain style of dance. It takes hours of hard work and dedication. It's amazing to see what the stars can pull off in a short amount of time.

Judges score the pair on how well they execute the dance, but it is up to the viewers to decide who stays and who goes. Will fans vote for their favorite celebrities who may not be skilled dancers, or will the best dancers **garner** the most votes?

Dancing Pros

Each season, many of the same professional dancers return to partner with a new cast of stars. Since the competition features new dances weekly, the pros have a lot of work to do. Not only do they have to whip the stars into shape, they must also choreograph the dances.

gymnast Laurie Hernandez, winner of season 23, and her dance partner

ted
ying
pace
cities
r the
vers.

range
stors.

vagen
 with
tt, an
rator.

pple's
ailing
ixing.

500m
velop
 cars.

now enough.

Tribute

Bindi Irwin (above), winner of season 21 of *Dancing with the Stars*, paid tribute to her father in some of her dances. Her father, Steve Irwin, was a nature expert and had his own reality show, *The Crocodile Hunter*. He died tragically while filming a documentary.

For most of these countries oil is the main source of

The Connection: TV and Social Media

Viewers of all types of TV, from reality to sporting events, get engaged with social media. It's a fun way to get involved in—and even have an impact on—the competition.

Sweet Tweets

More people use Twitter than Facebook to get social about their favorite series. In one week, 32 percent of Twitter activity was related to entertainment shows but only 18 percent of Facebook interactions were TV-related.

Most Tweeted Minute

The Voice fans voted on Twitter to save their favorite contestants from elimination during an "Instant Save." There were 217,000 tweets sent at 8:53 p.m. (EST) during the live semifinal results on December 8, 2015. This became the most tweeted minute for any episode of a show in the 2015–2016 season.

Sports Fans Unite

Sunday is the day with the most social media activity, with 43 percent of weekly Facebook interactions and 33 percent of Twitter activity. This is likely due to most people being home on Sunday and the major sporting events that air on this day.

REC

Money, Please

Another reason people may go on TV is for money. Some shows have people competing to win a top prize, which usually includes a large sum of money or a record deal. If you watch shows that follow people in their day-to-day lives, remember that they are getting paid to entertain you.

All in the Family

Some reality shows follow people's lives and are filled with drama. They are not always appropriate for audiences of all ages. However, there are some reality TV shows that the whole family can watch. Hidden camera and home video shows get laughs from audiences of all ages. Some talent competitions have kids and adults vying for a grand prize. Other shows feature actual families working together.

Families have tuned in to watch *America's Funniest Home Videos* for almost 30 years. Home videos that capture bloopers or funny kids and pets are sent in to the show. A host makes jokes and introduces the videos to a live audience.

It's fun to watch people of all ages show off their skills in the hope of winning a prize. Winners of *America's Got Talent* range from dog trainers to magicians to singers. Recent winners of the show have been kids!

Watch Worldwide

Some reality shows have spin-offs in other countries. The *Got Talent* franchise has shows in nearly 60 places, including countries in Europe, Africa, and the Middle East.

Other reality shows feature family members who share common interests. Watching them is a great way to come together and strengthen family bonds. Families can watch other families interact.

HGTV's *Property Brothers* stars a team of twin brothers. They help people find and create their dream homes. One brother, Drew, is a real estate agent, and the other brother, Jonathan, is a **contractor** who plans and executes the design of the home.

Fixer Upper features a husband-and-wife team, whose mission is to give people their dream homes. Chip and Joanna Gaines have an additional goal—making their small town a destination people want to visit and possibly call home.

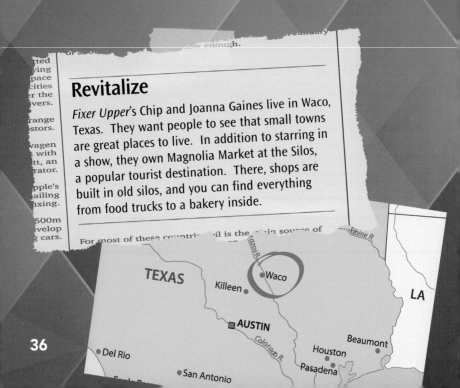

Revitalize

Fixer Upper's Chip and Joanna Gaines live in Waco, Texas. They want people to see that small towns are great places to live. In addition to starring in a show, they own Magnolia Market at the Silos, a popular tourist destination. There, shops are built in old silos, and you can find everything from food trucks to a bakery inside.

Brother Takeover

Drew and Jonathan Scott, the Property Brothers, have such a huge fan base that they have more than one show. On *Brother vs. Brother*, they each take on a renovation challenge and guest judges select the winner.

Other Reality Shows

Not all reality TV is about voting for a winner. Some shows are made simply for entertainment. They might show different lifestyles or expand your viewpoint.

Shark Tank

Dive into the world of business. A panel of "sharks," or business **moguls**, decide whether to invest in various companies. Watch as potential **entrepreneurs** pitch their business ventures to the sharks. A variety of businesses have been featured on the show, from cupcake businesses to bed bug detection companies.

House Hunters

Learn how people live all over the country. Watch as people find their dream homes. You will see everything from log cabins, to beach houses, to tiny houses.

Say Yes to the Dress

You don't have to be getting married to be interested in this show. Learn about different wedding customs and traditions. See brides search for a dress on a budget, or watch as a bride with no budget at all gets a fancy gown created just for her.

Your Reality

Being social is an essential part of daily life. One thing that can bring you, your peers, and even strangers together is a competition show. At school, you might connect with someone you didn't know before because of a shared interest in a show. You can communicate via social media about the competition as you watch it live. The next day, you can discuss what you saw, who you think should stay on the show, and who should go home.

tted
ying
pace
cities
r the
ivers.

range
stors.

vagen
with
tt, an
rator.

pple's
ailing
xing.

500m
velop
cars.

ow enough.

Get Social

One way to find others with similar interests is to search the hashtag for your favorite show. Many producers come up with these hashtags so that they can measure audience engagement with the show. So, go ahead and show support for your favorite show or contestant by using a hashtag on social media.

For most of these countri il is the in so of

You could even make it a competition between your friends. Whose favorite contestant will go the furthest or win the competition? Some people get very involved in the competition and are upset when their favorite people get voted off. But at the end of the day, it's all part of the fun of reality TV!

Instant Save

To get fans to keep their favorites around in *The Voice*, the hashtag #VoiceSave was created. This can save someone who is about to be eliminated. During one of the final rounds of the competition, people in the bottom three are eligible for this "Instant Save" from America.

Glossary

aired—was broadcast on television

alliances—unions between people or groups

applicants—people who apply to be chosen to participate in something

broadcast—transmit programs by television

compelling—able to keep your attention

condensed—made shorter through editing

contractor—a person who has a contract to provide materials or labor or to work a job

critique—to provide feedback about the good and bad parts of a performance

culinary—having to do with the kitchen or cooking

documentary—a TV show or film that gives facts about events or people

entrepreneurs—people who start their own businesses

era—a period of time

exotic—different or unusual

footage—unedited material recorded on film for the purpose of creating a show or movie

garner—to acquire by effort

genre—a type or category of literature or art

hobbies—interests or activities someone does for fun

hone—to make more effective

lavish—very rich, extravagant

mentor—an experienced and trusted advisor

misconception—a wrong idea about something

moguls—people of power, influence, or distinction

offshoot—something that develops from something larger

perfect—to make perfect

phenomenon—an event that is observed but may be hard to understand or explain

prominent—important and well-known

prowess—amazing skill

season—a period of time when a TV show is shown

textiles—fabrics

unscripted—not planned or written

vied—competed

Index

Check It Out!

Books

King, A. S. 2013. *Reality Boy*. Little, Brown Books for Young Readers.

MasterChef Junior. 2017. *MasterChef Junior Cookbook: Bold Recipes and Essential Techniques to Inspire Young Cooks*. Clarkson Potter.

McLaughlin, Emma, and Nicola Kraus. 2009. *The Real Real*. HarperCollins.

Websites

Candid Camera. www.candidcamera.com/.

"Cook Like A Master Chef Junior." www.fox.com /masterchef-junior/article/cook-like-a-masterchef-junior.

Videos

American Idol Tracker. www.latimes.com/entertainment /tv/showtracker/la-ca-0403-american-idol-performances-20160329-htmlstory.html.

Dancing with the Stars. abc.go.com/shows/dancing-with-the-stars/.

Try It!

You are a producer and are looking for the next big star. Create your own reality TV competition show. Make a storyboard to pitch to a network. What kind of competition will it be? What challenges will be included? How many contestants will there be? How will you edit the footage?

➤ How will your show be judged? Will audience votes be taken? Will there be any celebrity judges or guest appearances?

➤ You want to give the contestants as much help from mentors as possible. What guest stars will you bring on your show to help aspiring stars?

➤ Create a brochure that gives more information about your plans for the show.

About the Author

 Jordan Smith has worked in publishing for six years. She has watched reality TV for much longer. Her favorite reality shows include *America's Next Top Model* and *House Hunters*. When she's not checking in on the lives of reality stars, she can be found playing with her pups, Buzz and Bandit, at the beach.